rapture red & smoke grey

rapture red & smoke grey

by

sarah gordon

TURNSTONE PRESS

Turnstone Press
607-100 Arthur Street
Artspace Building
Winnipeg, MB
R3B 1H3 Canada
www.TurnstonePress.com

Turnstone Press gratefully acknowledges the assistance of The Canada Council for the Arts, the Manitoba Arts Council, the Government of Canada through the Book Publishing Industry Development Program, and the Government of Manitoba through the Department of Culture, Heritage and Tourism, Arts Branch, for our publishing activities.

The Canada Council for the Arts | Le Conseil des Arts du Canada

Manitoba Arts Council | Conseil des arts du Manitoba

Canada

Cover design: Tétro Design
Interior design: Sharon Caseburg
Printed and bound in Canada by Friesens for Turnstone Press.

National Library of Canada Cataloguing in Publication Data

Gordon, Sarah, 1977-
Rapture red & smoke grey / Sarah Gordon.

Poems.
ISBN 0-88801-285-3

I. Title. II. Title: Rapture red and smoke grey.

PS8563.O83636R36 2003 C811'.6 C2003-906488-3

This book is dedicated to Sue, Al, and John Gordon, and to anyone who has ever lived in the Newcastle apartment building on Assinibone Ave., Winnipeg.

Acknowledgements

I would like to thank Dennis Cooley, Dannell Ronald, Jo Snyder, Heidi Phillips, and the congregation of King's Fellowship.

Contents

rapture red & smoke grey

Winter in My City

the light that spills into my dark kitchen from the inside of the fridge.
the cold things preserved there. my silent rooms, their calm,
the last bus passing by my window at 4 a.m.,
one or two people sitting in the back.
the colour of cement in the morning, grey and pocked like the sky,
the stolen shopping carts under the bridge.
the salvation army sign that gives the wrong time and temperature,
and then says "with heart to God and hand to man."
a public fear of arson,
an obsession with fire and flood, the severity of winter,
department stores closing down, left cavernous.
the little jokes t.v. news anchors make, in the few seconds left
before the end of the hour.
night sirens sounding, bottles breaking, words scrawled on a wall
above a flurry of footprints.

Today is cold and damp in the bones as I was walking downtown the air was reaching through my jacket and sweater and I was prompted to write an essay on Egon Schiele's hands. They were cold like today, and searching, and were far, far too large. They did what they wanted, those hands, they were not mindful. They looked almost like x-rays. And of course when I say Egon Schiele's hands I mean his own flesh and blood which, I believe, continues to drip down all the drainpipes in Vienna, and I mean all the hands he ever painted on mothers, prostitutes, priests and little children and on death itself which never flew in on ragged wings as most deaths do, but felt for bodies under reams of black cloth. Hands rustling in shawls and cloaks and black silk frocks at funerals as church bells ring a scandal in the choir. My hands are sweating cold in my pockets and the city feels like a hunchback might, the snow is dirty and the birds are scavenging.

How odd to mention Vienna here, in the middle of a prairie winter location is everything. There's a lot of flat space and dirty white and so we leap to landmarks in the memory. The winter air searching like cold hands through my clothing reminds me of my trip to Vienna, the days in museums with Egon's white-knuckled bones, and in the very next room the golden-haired Klimt. Gustav's and Egon's paintings sharing the same wall, standing back to back, I suppose you could say like death and resurrection.

winter isn't pristine this year. it looks like faded apartment paint. fingerprints around the doorknobs and light switches and smudges on the cupboards. footsteps echo in the hall, leave traces of dirt and snow. nothing is frozen fully through and nothing is thawed either. no one remembers what day it is, there are no marching bands or banners just a soft grey hoarfrost in the trees that look blurry.

the colour of cement in the morning grey and pocked like the sky, a dead pigeon

one time I was leaving my apartment early in the morning for school and stepping off the curb I looked down and saw a dying pigeon. it was flapping its wings in a panic and then it just gave up suddenly and died. I'd never seen a dying pigeon before, a final flutter. I'd only seen dead ones. and I shouldn't even say saw it. I should say felt it dying. I felt its wings hitting me in the chest thrashing around inside and there was grit from the road all over—road salt and old snow and gravel, and then I heard it die, heard it give up and heard how still the air was after. and then I got really mad that it was a stupid dirty pigeon dying and I wanted to cry and curse that it's not worth it—all this feeling. it's not worth it at all.

And then God said to me

there is a thing called fearlessness
when your skin and your eyes
flash from one temperature to
another, and in the instant you
know you are capable of giving
over all your days and years—all minutes
of your living and dying and tearing
at things with your hands

for they are not yours anyway.

you are made of restraint, and
unrestraint, the space that breathes
between walls that heave and buckle.

you are made of tightening strings
as stretched on a violin that sings
and screeches a non-orchestra
of wild and hurting sound.

you are made of limits, and the few
steps just after them that feel so free
and uncareful

and you are made of retreat, and looking
back.

Do not look back, for there are things
stronger than fondness and regret—

there are things for you to tear down
and conquer, there are ruins to stand in
and weep over

the smoke that rises will billow long
through old windows

and then there will be
new work to do.

and just then the sun came up over my shoulder so i turned my head back to look and got hit in the corner of my eye with an arrow of light, the singe mark is still there. it hurts to see.

walking over the Donald bridge to work, watching my feet 'cause I forgot my glasses and it makes my head ache to watch the sky and the traffic and the signs and the frozen river. I know it all by heart anyway. the sky is softening this time of day and seems undecided. some cars have their headlights on and some don't. the big billboard on the corner says Parade of Homes and has a picture of a new house and a man-made lake with a fountain. the river is dirty white and marked with footprints, some kid's lost boot half-buried in the snow. would I miss this if I weren't here, would I bring this weak winter sky to mind—

you know what the problem with this place is?
there are no volcanoes.

sometimes I feel so loud, I feel too red. bright bright red bursting out everywhere. surging. and what if people knew that? what if I stained these sidewalks what if I spilled out onto the ice? the snow would turn red, the sky too, the tree-tops would look like exposed nerve endings and everyone would be sobbing their guts out for once, out in the open though.
no. more. pale. sky.

the pioneers didn't know many pale skies. they knew fierce skies, storm skies, merciless bright white skies, burning skies, starry skies. stars did not blink or wink back then. stars were painful. they winced. on and off and on and off and on until beaten they fell.

and the grass grit their teeth and grew, and the stones turned and the ground gave.

the pioneers knew certain things.
what they knew:

—your weakness is for the dogs to tear apart and eat.

—whenever you cry for yourself you are wasting water.

—everything you own is flammable. (the smell of smoke your burning makes)

—there are forces that unmake you and everything you've built. your architecture. your house coming apart, like hands.

—tar is black and sticky and is made of humiliation used for roads and fixing leaky roofs.

—when God grabs your face to get your attention he leaves tarry fingerprints on your jaw.

the pioneers knew how to stand without the aid of shelters or bivouacs, how to sleep uncurled in the open. they knew not to tie rags to their nightmares, lest they attract wind's breath to live there like a flag.

they knew that efforts often flail. they knew that violence and tenderness are the same animal beaten soft, they knew to stroke the underbelly.

they knew that it's okay to be upset that the snow is dirty and the birds are scavenging—because that's not how things are supposed to be.

and they knew that beneath every word you speak there is a thin grey shadow that slips in and steals meaning, puts it to sleep with a silent executioner's grin.

when the pioneers came to clear the land they did not come with stealth or creeping on silent paws. theirs were blunt axes and dull swords swung wildly to hit trees and tear them out.

if I get to the base of things, of desire, all I really want to do is sing, and run. to sing well and loud, to run tirelessly, to be thoroughly exhausted with good work done.

that is what I want.

to know who God is, and how he works, and what his hands and eyes look like, and fire.

whenever I think of cement I think of neon red letters because there's a whole lot of cement downtown but then there's the salvation army sign I can see from my kitchen window. past the dumpsters and across the parking lot. big red letters that scroll across and say *with heart to God and hand to man* or *God loves you* or *Red Shield Brigade.* I look at it every morning to see what the message is. and I listen for the rattling of shopping carts stolen the night before.

we all need red messages to read. they are as essential as red pylons around a man-hole. we all need dead pigeons we need to know what final flutter means, that last up-surge of life we should feel it all the time we should be always trying like that.

the tension of weapons is something we could all use, as we seem to have lost the muscles that allow us to reach forward, straining beyond our normal capacity. rarely do we grimace out of sheer effort, rarely do we collapse from trying so hard. by tension of weapons I mean the stretch and pull of a slingshot. the pull back and let go, the soaring, the purpose and point of an arrow. the switchblade flies open, the hair-trigger so sensitive the slightest touch will discharge the bullet inside. if we could be weapons our teeth would be sharper, we would be more hungry, we would feel force and motion and purpose inside, we would fly, be bendable, be useful and dangerous, we would propel ever onward, never get tired.

What I fear, at the base of my spine, the pit in my stomach is that my body will fail, my wrists give out so that I drop what I'm carrying. I fear for the arches in my feet, my eyes.

what if what if
I never get to know who God is, and how he works, and his hands and his eyes and fire.

Outgoing Mail, a series of postcards

postcard to Christopher Pratt.

Dear Sir, as you can see winter is not pristine this year, but thank you for trying. I am worried that you try too hard to make the snow perfect and the shadows etched but I wouldn't have you any other way, just know that I am concerned. You know they did a documentary on you and the best scene was with you outside in the wind angrily folding and bending your bad proofs into the trash can and lighting them on fire. Something was not right in them you said, a spot in a spotless room, the wrong shade of clean, a crease in the landscape, the bed, or simply some dust getting in the beam. The can was bright blue and the flames orange and the paper these crisp white angles and it was entirely indelicate and real, and Christopher, what I want to say is, there are things that are spoiled in the north there are footprints of noise that march right through. So if you could paint some bigger paintings, or, at least let your figures have some warmth or hue, they are getting cold. Firelight is wasted on burning your mistakes.

Respectfully yours,
Sarah Gordon

postcard to Anne Carson.

Dear Anne. I am writing in response to the Afterword you wrote for part three of *Plainwater*. You are right, and I thank you for directly addressing me. When the paint on the story dried, I was left to contend with the pain of a recent injury to my lower back. I was propped up with pillows, and it was my birthday and I was alone in the house with the clock ticking loudly from its corner, and the second after I read about the bones in the wounds, I thought about volcanoes and red and lava heaving out of ragged holes, and I felt weak and impaled but I knew that my blood was searching through my body anyway, in spite of my pale skin. There was a brief vision of dark blood waves spilling up onto white sands, and your calm acknowledgement of this helped to ease the nausea of that moment. In all of us there is a lifewish. Our blood is insistent on this, even when we are flat on our backs on our birthdays. I appreciate your audacity, and your adjectives that come closer to naming the truth than any I have read. If I were the type to gush, I would sign this letter differently. However, I will sign it
—with strength and reserve, Sarah.

postcard to Michael Ondaatje.

Hello again. I was just wondering if you knew the artist Joseph Beuys. (He fell out of a plane too, and was kept alive by nomads who wrapped his injured body in felt cloth and animal fat.) Some say it's a myth, but I know you believe that myths can be true. Besides political speeches, Joseph never spoke, except to coyotes, and sometimes to dead rabbits though then he only mouthed the words. There are many photographs of him standing in corners, I think to support the room. I was hoping, if you knew him, that you might write a book about him, for there are some things I'd like to know. If you need a place to start, there are, of course, the sealed letters and burnt doors, but there is also Maria Abramovic, whom I saw in a photo with him, and who was in the habit of scrubbing skeletons. She might be good to talk to because she once screamed for three hours straight before losing her voice. If you end up making a movie, I think Helena Bonham Carter and Willem Defoe. They are both wily. I might warn you though, that there seems to be nothing subtle, everything is blunt and raw so the actors may be uncomfortable at times. Let me know what you think. —Sarah Gordon postcard to Robert Motherwell.

dear Mr. Motherwell. I am writing in response to your elegies. unfortunately for me, there are none in my city, and so I'm forced to look them up in books, or go back in my mind to Chicago, where I saw my first elegy in person. I am also reminded of them whenever I see an oil slick, or a pool of tar on new cement. and there are plenty of black asphalt roads running through snowy fields around here. in the darkroom I wave my hand in front of my face and cannot see it, I've disappeared, a train stopped deep in a tunnel by hijackers and held hostage there. if you make it out alive there's that first squint of light that hurts your eyes. but I guess the point is we don't make it out alive, we forget how to swim. we're blotted out, we become absent. everyone should have an elegy in their home, a black hole they cannot ignore hanging on their wall. each day at five o'clock in the afternoon they should turn and face it and look and remember. I pray you never have a retrospective—imagine all the elegies in one room, imagine standing in the middle. I don't think I could handle it, the black would take over. if you're the coalminer I'm the daughter. respectfully, Sarah Gordon.

postcard to partygoers.

Dear friends, how I wish things could be different. I was sitting in the sunroom last night, watching you draw little drawings in the window frost with your fingers, watching you smoking and tipping the glass to your lips every so often saying something funny, and I was very fond of you then when we locked eyes and grins and you sat on my feet so they wouldn't get cold. And I sat there still, when the room changed as it does at every party, when words get rough around the edges, a little explosive, and grins start to crack wider, and looks turn into glances, and tensions become visible, stretching as tight and dangerous as elastics between us. And if we survive that hour, we sit there longer and longer, too tired to get up and go home to bed, and the sunroom becomes soft and lazy like a drawl, and we're all a little shy or embarrassed about something we might've said. And I watched you then, and your eyes were black though you didn't know it you were the life and death of that party. And if things were different I would have told you that I loved you, that I was concerned for all the days of your life, that I was hopeful and tired and sad. And on the cold walk home I would have named out loud all the terrible things that assault you, or reached in your throat and pulled them out to spill on the snow before us. —S.

postcard to Jane Urqhuart.

dear Jane. I haven't yet read your new book *The Stone Carvers,* though I must tell you I'm nervous to read it. I have that feeling in my stomach. It's very awkward to walk around all day with this feeling, with this staggered heartbeat, with this shifting around of things inside to make room for your words. I expect to be changed, somehow, again. Reading your books is like rigorous exercise, I feel all stretched out and sore afterwards. I feel collapsed and wanting, and for some reason, I really notice knuckles after reading your books, how they turn white when I clench them, how the tiny folds of skin pull tight and then slacken when I rest. And of course I notice the ribcages of young men, all their slim bones nudging, and I must admit this makes me jealous. Women must express themselves in other ways, we must make startling, quick gestures that sound like stabs. We must burn things or break delicate things or twist the necks of birds and then fall sobbing upon them. Or, we must collect all these gestures into words and wait, with painful patience, until they're born. Thank you for writing.
Sincerely, Sarah Gordon

postcard to Anthony Hopkins.

I am concerned about actors. They are a strange phenomenon to me, they must be all stretched out of shape inside like silly putty, or, have in them a large and immovable slab of stone that keeps them grounded. You, for example, have acted such extremes. To think of C.S. Lewis and Dr. Lecter sharing the same body and voice is, to me, perplexing. And where does that leave you? Perhaps you are most like the butler you played in *Remains of the Day*, always evasive and non-committal, preferring to stick to the script. I hope you are not so disappointing, I hope you listen to the words coming out of your acting mouth with your own real ears and respond to them in some way. I hope you are more loyal to yourself than to the people whose lives you've lived for awhile, on screen. You see, sir, I have been to the fields of Oxford where you walked in Lewis' shoes, and the air was soft there, and there were horses breathing. I've never been to the other set, except in nightmares, and I don't like thinking of you there. Landscapes, I think, can be very influential. And in my mind, it is better to live in sorrow than in lawlessness. Please take care of yourself, your profession demands it.
Respectfully, Sarah Gordon

Poems written mid January

I.

in the turn your body makes while waking,
your blood sloshes its secrets over the side

tipping out like a boat the sluggish warmth
of sleep, spilling on the floor.

(you went to bed unhappy again,
sick even, a lurching in you, a fishhook snag)

you make coffee and toast,
the kettle whistle a thin scream
in the cold kitchen.

II.

in the white light of winter
the sky is a lock
fastened on your forehead
a featureless white field where men
with cold and clumsy fingers struggle
to set fires in the hush of snow

where dark shapes lie
curled on the ice, in stiff black coats
of coarsened skin,
their blackened fingers fierce
and frozen in you.

III.

cold is made of beauty and fear
and thaw is made of aching.

the pain in your own hands,
blood surging sore in them

like yanking red ribbons.

IV.

somewhere
a fire, wanting, rages
through your house.

flames lick the boards and timbers,
lick out of you every corner
of room

like glory breathing
into wood.

V.

icefish thaw in your sink, scoured. silver fin, eye bright.

the last threads of evening are frayed gold.
you make dinner. as you move around the kitchen
the word *glorious* burns you from the inside
as an old stove warms slow to its edges

you wince and laugh closer to it.

night's windows turn you away,
reflect only what's behind you, rooms
where you pace, where you wait
trapped inside your discomfiture
—your discomfiture,
because you own it, a desire to feel
even the minor vibrations
of the earth, detectable only
on delicate measuring instruments.

you want more
than what you bargained for.
in your dreams seismologists on t.v. warn
of weak points along faults and fissures, cut
to scenes of alert animals,
tensed and ready to run.

sidewalks crack, split
the ground heaves, heavy
objects crash to the floor
from high shelves shards of
glassware fall, bottles and china
trembling there

you surrender, give yourself over
to a slow unmaking
of everything you've built, your architecture,
your house coming apart (like hands),

the boom of collapsed corridors
resounding

in the aftermath, broken
cables spark in the shocked street
gas and fluid leak from car bodies
quiet now you wait, and see
what still lies there, whispering.

a long silence, and then the words

there are things that cannot be shaken

all blood has a cry.

stay away from windows and mirrors,
avoid trees and masonry,
avoid elevators and staircases,
they attract panicking people,
crawl carefully.

warmth is the weight of an animal sleeping
on your body at night,
and cold is that animal leaving.

in winter
warmth is only a visitor.

and cold is what builds you into a house
against the wind.

fire is what claws you
awake with a searing
in your skin.

beauty is not enough,

it fails real hunger
of the stomach where
there is a ragged hole
of wanting, where
there is lack.

the shining world pretends.
the world makes things
that are beautiful,
screens flicker on our faces
and on our pillows at night

though they do not
splatter us with blood
or maul open our throats,

we do that on our own.

and we are sorry

for the holes of hunger
we gape through

for all the red throats leaking
warmth on the scenery.

if I die an angry beautician's death,
let my last words be

it was not enough,

nothing the world gave
was enough.

Pilgrimage to Kansas City

Inside a pilgrim's rucksack there would be very few items. There would, of course, be matches, preferably waterproofed because young, inexperienced pilgrims cry a lot and this tends to dampen things. There would also be a needle and thread to mend torn clothing and some salve to soothe holes made by arrows and darts, and there might be a small vial to collect wild honey and a dropper for wine. However, the most pious do not believe in storage. Bread is not an issue, as most paths have along them many large loaf-shaped stones. The one luxury item would be a tin cup for drinking, the silver surface would become dull with fingerprints and every so often the pilgrim would get to polish it clean and shining. Some feeble-voiced pilgrims carry with them a megaphone for announcements, warnings, and proclamations, and others carry searchlights. The only other thing I can think of is tent pegs, though some opt to sleep in the open with the word of God a blazing banner over them, the letters flaming louder than stars.

South Dakota highway
we entered the nation of promises some time ago, the sky over us
a snowdome, strangely lit. billboards become beacons in this light,
power lines hum along repeating fields of snow, every so often a
thin skiff of last year's grass. words start small, grow larger and
appear in the car window, "welcome to Watertown Dakota's rising
star this exit"

on the highway I look for things that match me, that match what I
am. certain billboards stark in colour against the snow or stark
against bland damp grass trampled by fields of frozen water. the red
billboard, the sound of gravel hitting the car.

if you were a truck what would you haul? heating & cooling
equipment.

entering Kansas City it is dusk and the streetlights turn on in shifts, the freeway's slow and easy, downtown is deserted. but there are nests in the trees we marvel over, why are there so many? I blink and the branches become arteries and the nests clots. where are the birds dark like stitches?

it is a grand hotel with revolving doors and a silver buffet in the lobby, a handsome valet. our room on the 17th floor. we weren't expecting such a tragic view, the city of fountains and smashed ruby shoes

sad like trashy red glitter
in the eyes of birds
who can't find anything else to eat.

money has a desperate smell
cold like cement of an underground parkade
below a fancy hotel

on a pilgrimage everything counts, everything that happens is a kind of omen. there are secret messages in cities, well disguised in signs and street names. today I walked down Perishing Road, heard an old man muttering about elevators except he kept calling them Lifts and Downs.

hanging in the lobby are some very heavy, very expensive
chandeliers. what if the cord stretches and snaps—
a million glass bulbs smash on the floor
in the flash of a photograph, blackout.

when traveling in America there is often the feeling that something is very wrong. there is a pervading sense of doom, even in springtime. the word *doom* rolls in like thunder, rolls slow like a big grey boulder, echoes into place.

there are prophets in Kansas City who see plane crashes in their minds before they happen, except they get to see them in slow motion. they see sports arenas on fire, feel the tremors of earthquakes, see blood spots on snow. apparently an earthquake hits you in the stomach first, just before the first tremor it knocks you from the inside so your guts get loose.

there is something about experiencing another city's spring when
your own city is locked in winter that feels a little like adultery.
watching something awaken is a very intimate thing, you almost
want to look away.
I sat on the soggy grass and watched the grit melt off my shoes.
the fountains had not yet come on and I was glad for I thought that
might be overdoing it a little.
there were small disturbances of air where birds had just been and
the statues were dirty and impatient. omens were everywhere again.
why are omens louder in America or am I just starting to believe in
advertising?

in the big grey convention center next to our hotel there is a religious rally going on, there are escalators to take you up and down, and a place to buy T-shirts and keepsakes and inspired words. preachers scream into microphones until their throats go hoarse and all the girls cry little diamond-shaped tears that sparkle in the light and women gone raw on the inside claw the air and flap their arms like struggling birds while the men raise anguished faces to heaven and some of them double over. then there's a blast of trumpets and a gust of wind and the preacher calls up anyone with heart disease and thousands of black and bitten and shriveled hearts with holes surge forward and I strain to hear the murmuring of them, the skipped beats. but the microphones are ringing in my ears and I can't hear—

it kind of hurts it seems rash and careless why does God make our bodies so violently able to be cleft open like that—

outside the evening is cool and empty, there is a discernible lack of fervor in the air. on the walk back to the hotel I build myself back into me, leaving gaps in the planks so questions can get through like do I have a heart of stone will God strike will water flow you see we don't use our bodies properly, a prophet was saying to someone in the elevator. for example, if you ever open your throat completely, it almost always makes a war-cry.

had a shower to calm down, pulled the curtain between me and the rest of the world, thankful the hotel had the foresight not to use those transparent shower curtains that let you still see blurry shapes, stretching new muscles and concentrating on nothing but the beige tiles and swirling drain but couldn't stop myself from thinking about the place where all the pipes from all the drains in the hotel connect into one giant drain and where does that go? it must bubble up somewhere.
got out and the bathroom floor was under an inch of water, my clothes all wet. I hadn't pulled the curtain in all the way. I bent naked, sopping up water with white hotel towels and thought how many times have I done this before, wading through shallow lakes of my own making.

my throat's all stretched out like how it feels when you wake up crying, a strange sadness heavy on your chest.

there's a row of trees along the convention center you know how they look like they're growing out of cement? it was really strange one night real late there were blackbirds there, never seen so many in one place before, hundreds in each tree still as silhouettes, kind of ominous and beautiful though like brushstrokes somehow. I wouldn't have seen them it was so dark and the street lamps had already faded but I heard a shifting in the trees and looked up and there they were and I forgot I had been wondering about them all along. you know like when you've lost something and spend all day looking and suddenly it's just sitting right there in front of you, silent and black and edgy I thought, they were hard to see in the dark, they were ragged little black holes torn out of black paper and I wondered what would the prophets say about them, what sign are they?

so I spent all night chewing on words in my sleep trying to get the meaning of the word *black*, but I grind my teeth so when I woke up in the morning the *b* was bitten off and I was left with *lack* and I remembered my dream of a mouthful of cavities. and I knew then that there are black holes everywhere. blackbird holes, black eye holes, wet black puddle holes and the little holes black words make in our mouths.
black holes up in us, takes what's there and leaves lack.

there's a lot of people staying here, there are line-ups shuffling in and out of elevators stopping on every floor.

an elevator is a small mirrored chamber that can carry you up and down, if you look in the mirror you continue on and on and on. there's a red button that says FIRE. press when ready to be consumed. there's a rumour going round that there are prophets on the third floor hidden in secret rooms.

the birds come every night now, leaving a white mess on the sidewalk and cars. they're getting noisier too. they have thin high voices that tangle together and some are getting into attics, garages—one was found strangled in a mess of old wires. if your room's below the attic and the walls are thin you can hear them rummaging in your forgotten things.

you know it hurts to move a dead bird, a strange weight carried in your hands. small birds that hit windows weigh only a bundle of thread but bigger birds weigh heavy. you feel it in the pit of your stomach when you pick them up and try to fold their awkward wings. some die in winter and are buried under snow but it's spring now and everything is melting. and still they surprise you when you find one, you jump back a little when you catch its eye. in spring the world comes back and this makes you mad the things that come out of the ice.

it's fish Friday at the silver-dish buffet you can smell it in the halls. you see tiny white fish bones lodging in throats. something smells fishy is the joke in the elevator, nervous laughter.

sign and wonder count: blackbird, billboard, crystal chandelier, fish bones, fire option.

the birds are gone. they cut down every second tree and amputate the rest. the air rings, unnerved. where will they go now, pushed out of the city by owners of cars, where will they fly? reporters gather in the felled trees and severed limbs, their long coats blowing in the wind. all the toppled nests—

the word *doom* was resounding again and we didn't know what to do so we went dancing in the hotel lounge and I've never danced so hard before. some of the prophets requested *Great Balls of Fire* with a wry smile. the pianist was a passionate man he played with his heart banging the keys, his heart a bludgeon beating on them, the music almost fell apart the tables and chairs were shaking.

my body woke up a collection of new pains, more new muscles aching with first use. I'd been working all night stopping leaks and filling holes and felling trees and folding birds and not to mention dancing.

getting out of bed I feel a smaller pain wedged strangely in my body, on an angle or something that cuts slightly into my breathing—

there's no trace the birds were ever here, the sidewalk's washed, the tree limbs carried away.

on the highway again, new grass fields stand and salute as we pass by. pay attention to the billboards, there are still unanswered questions. thank you for visiting Kansas City. city of fountains. city of spring.

First Breath of Spring

why can't all our words be strong, why can't they sing.
because, you tell me, there is too much mess in spring.
spring is sluggish.
and this makes me angry. mud and slush
and last year's trampled grass and
stray mittens caught in the bushes by the bus stop
and the bus windows are splattered so dirty grey
you can't see out.

we should all be angry.
our city's not waking up it's sleeping in.

there's a better language, a pure one.

there are words so clean and precise it hurts to say them out loud,
they scald the mouth,
they wedge, they ricochet, and ravage soft surfaces
words so intricate and exact they are spiky little motors,
tiny splinter machines whirling and hurling—

and there are words that stun like a blow to the head, an axe in the gut, a cleaver in the heart.

words fail
like the human heart
without God to defend it.

there's cool night air breathing on my face and the hollow of my throat as I walk home from a friend's house at 2 a.m. and looking down over the bridge I see the ice is breaking apart on the river, finally spring is breaking open and for some reason my mind flashes forward to the future, and I nearly double over from the pain of it and there's a smile stretching on my face from the hope of it and a new ache begins called joy, I think. and these are big words, pain and hope and joy, but I can handle them just barely and the ice isn't shattering or splintering or sharding. there's no small fragments, no mess. these are quick clean breaks, they are sudden, and that's the most painful thing. when a crack starts creeping slow and suddenly there's black river water swelling between the two split parts of you and there's a slight throb in the air and you can't bear it, except you know that these are the moments we're supposed to beg for. we must not desire them we must want them. and when they come we must want more.

you can't kill words. and you can't kill me you bastard because

there are anthems in the air, there are reasons
to raise hands
and fists

and flags and sails.

there is the beauty of watching things collide in slow motion.

there are the unbearable things.

and the changing of weather.

there is the word *yet* running through our veins,

there is tireless dancing
there is the very first moment a song ignites a crowd

when that sickened bird-dead place in us
revives.